technology and you

Internet History

Donna Loughran

www.raintreepublishers.co.uk
Visit our website to find out more information about **Raintree** books.

To order:
- ☎ Phone 44 (0) 1865 888112
- 🖹 Send a fax to 44 (0) 1865 314091
- 🖥 Visit the Raintree Bookshop at www.raintreepublishers.co.uk to browse our catalogue and order online.

First published in Great Britain by Raintree, Halley Court, Jordan Hill, Oxford OX2 8EJ, part of Harcourt Education. Raintree is a registered trademark of Harcourt Education Ltd.

Editorial: Nick Hunter and Catherine Clarke
Design: Tower Design
Picture Research: Maria Joannou
Production: Jonathan Smith

Originated by Dot Gradations Ltd
Printed and bound in China by South China Printing Company

ISBN 1 844 21721 3
07 06 05 04 03
10 9 8 7 6 5 4 3 2 1

British Library Cataloguing in Publication Data
Loughran, Donna
Internet History.–(Technology and you)
004.6'78'09
A full catalogue record for this book is available from the British Library.

Acknowledgements
The publishers would like to thank the following for permission to reproduce photographs: Alamy Images pp. **4**, **6**; Aurora p. **5** (Michael Wolf); Collections (Mike Kipling) p. **23**; Corbis pp. **11** (Eric Curry), **13** (Lawrence Manning), **14** (Bettmann), **15** (Bettmann), **30** (Roger Ressmeyer), **31** (AFP); EAC Images/Nasa/Aurora pp. **12**, **22**; Image Bank p. **42**; Oxfam International p. **34**; Science Photo Library p. **18**.

Additional photography, including cover, by Comstock Royalty Free; Corbis Royalty Free and Getty Images Royalty Free.

The publishers would like to thank Michael Hurley for his assistance in the preparation of this book.

Every effort has been made to contact copyright holders of any material reproduced in this book. Any omissions will be rectified in subsequent printings if notice is given to the publishers.

Contents

Any words appearing in the text in bold, **like this**, are explained in the Glossary.

What is the Internet?

Have you heard about the Internet and wondered what it is? Do you use the Internet but wonder how and when it all began?

The Internet is a huge computer **network**. In a way, it is a network of networks. When it began, in the 1960s, the network had only four computers. Today, it is a network made up of millions of computers.

What is a network? A network is a group of connected people or things. Imagine people all over the world linked together, holding hands. The Internet is something like that.

One way to think of the Internet is as a network of computer networks.

In this case, the Internet is a network of computers and the people who use them. It stretches around the world,

connected by telephone and television lines, and cables and communications satellites. A satellite is a device that moves around Earth in space and receives and **transmits** messages from and to all parts of the world.

The Internet is mainly a communication network, which means you can use it to share information.

Think of the Internet as a web of roads and motorways. In fact, the Internet has been called an 'information superhighway'.

Telephone and television wires are the main roads of the information superhighway system known as the Internet.

The Internet allows you to find information, share ideas with people around the world and 'visit' other countries, without ever leaving home.

Surfing the Internet

As an Internet 'traveller' or 'surfer' you can play games, send email to friends, or search for information on any subject you can think of. If you don't have anything in particular that you want to find out about, you can just 'surf', or look around. When you are connected to the Internet – you are online.

Today, the Internet links nearly every country in the world.

Although the Internet began in the USA, it is now a source of information and a form of communication for people all over the world. Each day, more and more people are using the Internet.

What does a network look like?

Computer **networks** come in all shapes and sizes. A diagram of them may look like interconnected lines, circles, or webs. The number of connected computers, or **hardware**, determines a network's size and shape. Hardware is the name given to the computers, cables, or other equipment used to make the system work.

*This technician is working on the hardware of a **server**, which is a large computer that stores information for a network.*

People who design networks think about several things. First, they think about the people who will use it. What do they need? What technology, or tools, can help them? Designers also think about the location of the network hardware. For example, are the computers to be connected in the same room or different rooms? What if the computers are in different buildings or different countries even? All these things must be considered in the design of a network.

Simple and complex networks

A **network** can be as small as two computers connected in a way that allows them to share information.

A local network in a small office might include four computers and one printer. Cables connect the computers to each other and to the printer. This allows the people using these four computers to share their information. They can also all use the same printer.

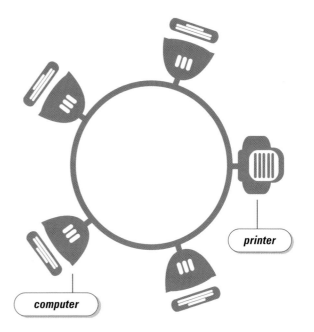

computer

printer

The diagram above shows a basic network. In this case four computers and a printer make up the network.

Many computers and printers can be linked to a central computer or **server** – usually through a **hub**. The server manages access to the information stored on the network and allows the computers connected to it to share that information.

Some larger companies also share information using an **Intranet**. This works in a similar way to the Internet, but is only available within a company or organization, to people who are connected to that company's network.

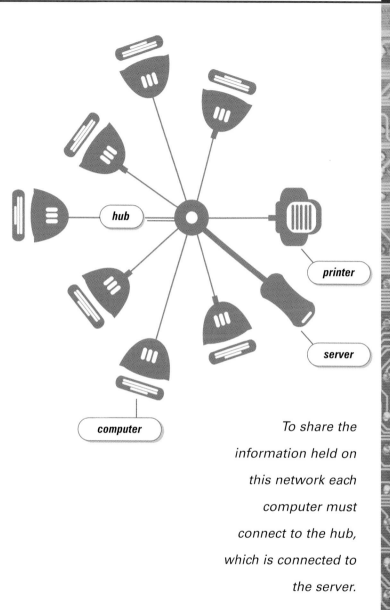

To share the information held on this network each computer must connect to the hub, which is connected to the server.

9

Other communication networks

The Internet uses **telecommunication networks**, which are the connected systems of cables, wires and satellites used to communicate over great distances.

A telephone network is one kind of telecommunication network. You may have noticed that most people use a telephone line to connect to the Internet. Early telephone networks could carry only voice messages. Today, they can carry video, music, pictures and other information.

Technology has advanced to the point where a mobile telephone can be used to access the Internet.

Television networks form another kind of telecommunication network. Television networks broadcast, or send, information in one direction.

However, today these broadcast systems are becoming interactive. This means that messages can flow in both directions.

This two-way communication is made possible by special cable and satellite systems. It is these same systems that let us connect our computers to the Internet.

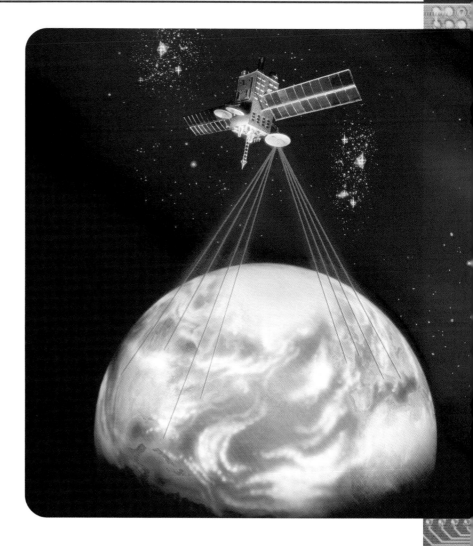

*This illustration shows how a communications satellite in space can receive and **transmit** signals and information from and to different places around the world.*

Networks within networks

Early computers were huge. They were so large that they filled up rooms. These huge computers, called **mainframes**, had to be kept cool – otherwise they could get too hot to work.

Today, the Internet depends on desktop or personal computers. Such computers are designed to be owned and used by individuals – fitting comfortably on the top of a desk. These computers are much smaller than mainframes, but they can store lots of data, or information. In fact, a single desktop computer is more powerful than the giant computers of the past. It can also process more information, faster.

The first computers needed an enormous amount of space and used up a tremendous amount of energy.

The Internet is a **network** of millions of smaller networks. The networks use **servers** to store information or provide services such as email.

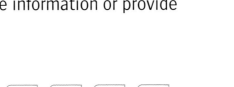

Telephone wires made from copper and glass connect the computers of a network, or even connect networks. The glass wires are called fibre-optic telephone cables. Coaxial cable, a special braided wire, is a kind of cable that carries television signals and also links computers. Satellites can also carry these signals. Computers change the signals carried by these systems into a language they can recognize.

The language of computers is used to create programs, or **software**. It takes both **hardware**, such as computers and cables, and software to make the Internet work.

Fibre-optic cable consists of a bundle of glass threads, each of which can communicate messages.

Beginning of the Internet

The Internet began in the late 1950s and early 1960s. The president of the USA, President Dwight D. Eisenhower, had asked the US Department of Defense to find a faster way to communicate. He wanted people in government, research and military organizations to be able to share information.

After commanding the Allied invasion of Normandy that helped bring the Second World War to an end, Dwight D. Eisenhower was president of the USA from 1953 to 1961.

The wizards of ARPANET

Eisenhower's request went to the Advanced Research Projects Agency (ARPA) of the US federal government. ARPA's purpose was to make scientific discoveries for the military. Some of ARPA's researchers were well-known scientists. Some were called 'wizards' because they had taught themselves about computers and computer programming. Others were called 'nerds' and 'geeks' because they spent all of their time building computers and writing computer programs.

A computer scientist at work in the 1950s, the dawn of the 'Computer Age'.

Many of these researchers were a bit **eccentric**. One **software** designer came to work barefoot. Many forgot to sleep as they spent endless days working on new ways to use computers. All of these researchers had something in common – they saw the importance of computers to the future. They dreamed about a world community connected by a **network** of computers.

In 1966, a man called Bob Taylor became the director of ARPA. At the time, there were several large, **mainframe** computers around the USA, but ARPA needed more. One computer, called SAGE, was so large that people could walk inside it. Another took up several rooms. These giant computers were expensive to build and expensive to run. So Bob Taylor came up with another idea.

Telephone lines allow people to connect to the Internet from home, school or work.

Taylor decided to try making an electronic link, or **network**, between these giant computers. That way, researchers doing similar work in different parts of the country could share their results. They could also share the costs of computer time. Before Taylor's idea would work, however, he needed a new design for a communication network.

People have always found a way to communicate. They have also found ways to communicate faster.

By the middle of the 20th century, the telephone network had become the fastest way to send messages. Yet, for ARPA, this was still not good enough. What Taylor and others like him – computer designers and engineers such as Paul Baran in the USA and Donald Davies in the UK – wanted was to build a computer network that would work like a human brain.

The brain sends messages through the nervous system. In a sense, the nervous system is like a huge network **transmitting** information around the body.

Techno Tip

In 1784 John Palmer set up the first horse drawn mail coach service in the world. This service relied on quick changes of horses to reach average speeds of just 8 miles per hour. Today, an email can reach its destination – thousands of miles across the world – within seconds. With technology advancing all the time – who knows what may be possible in the future?

Baran and Davies thought they could design a computer **network** that worked in the same way. Along the telephone networks of the time, messages travelled slowly on a single path. A computer network that worked like a human brain could move more messages and move them faster.

Baran and Davies thought that computers could divide information or messages up into chunks, called packets. Packets could flow through many network pathways.
When they reached where they were going, the receiving computers could put the packets together again.

A new network design was only a piece of the puzzle. If people were going to connect computers to share information, the computers would have to 'speak' the same language.

Scientists have tried to make computers work like the human brain – one of the most amazing communications networks ever!

Bob Taylor knew that different computers used different languages, or **software**. Computers that used different languages could not share information. Taylor faced a huge challenge. Even if he could design a network to connect computers, how was he going to get the computers to understand each other?

Wes Clark, another computer engineer, had an idea. Why not build smaller computers that all spoke the same software language? These smaller computers, called 'imps,' would be connected to the **mainframe** computers located around the country. The imps would take messages from the mainframes and translate those messages into a language that other computers could understand.

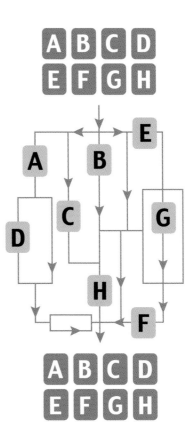

On a network, a computer message is broken into packets and put back together on the receiving computer.

19

Ben Barker worked with the imps. His job was to 'debug' them. This means he had to make sure they worked when the power was switched on. If they didn't work, he had to find the problem, or 'bug,' and fix it.

Will Crowther led the **software** design team. Its mission was to write the software, or language, that would allow the imps to communicate with the **mainframes**.

*When talking about computers, a bug is something that interferes with the proper running of a program, machine or **network**.*

Crowther was a rock climber as well as an engineer. He liked to wear comfortable clothes and trainers to work. He also liked to hang from the doorways in his office while he made up computer programs in his head.

After years of research, experiments and models, the first imps were put to work. Imps were installed and connected

to three mainframe computers in California and one in Utah.

When the imps succeeded in translating simple messages from the giant computers,the programmers and designers cheered. It might seem like a small step now, but Bob Taylor and his group of researchers had the Advanced Research Projects Agency Network, or ARPANET, up and running. Soon it would begin to connect computers in military and government bases all over the world.

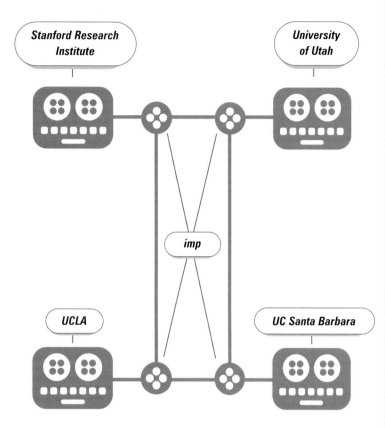

The ARPANET was the first step towards the Internet as we know it today. Established in 1969, it was the first large, wide-area computer network.

21

Scientists and teachers join in

Soon, non-military government groups, like the National Aeronautics and Space Administration (NASA), joined the ARPANET. Teachers, researchers and scientists also began to see the value of a computer network like this. They understood that ARPANET could connect people all over the world and that these people could share new and exciting ideas. The information they shared could spark new and important scientific discoveries.

Mission control at the NASA space centre in Houston, USA, is where engineers and scientists monitor space flights. Space exploration would be impossible without advanced computer technology.

By this time, some universities, like the University of California and the University of Michigan, had begun developing their own email and computer **networks**. In 1969, researchers at four universities used telephones to link their computer networks. In the mid-1970s, the US government invited various science organizations to join the ARPANET.

In 1979, the US National Science Foundation (NSF), a group of teachers and scientists, started its own network, called the Computer Science Net (Csnet). In 1982, the US Department of Defense and the NSF created a link that allowed ARPANET and Csnet to exchange information.

Research and development of Internet technology is still going on at universities all over the world.

23

Opening the door to the world

By the mid-1980s, many other smaller **networks** had begun around the world. A series of procedures, called 'Internetworking protocol' allowed these networks to join with ARPANET. They also gave a name to the new, larger network that was formed – the Internet.

Internet engineers came up with a special language that all computer networks could understand. This common language is called HTML, which stands for Hypertext Markup Language.

HTML is the computer language that allows you to access millions of different sites on the World Wide Web.

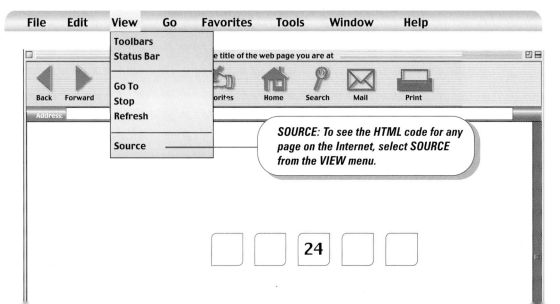

| File | Edit | View | Go | Favorites | Tools | Window | Help |

Toolbars
Status Bar

Go To
Stop
Refresh

Source

e title of the web page you are at

Back   Forward   orites   Home   Search   Mail   Print

Address:

SOURCE: To see the HTML code for any page on the Internet, select SOURCE from the VIEW menu.

24

The letters 'http' in an Internet address, or URL (see page 29), stand for hypertext. The 'http' is one computer letting another computer know that they are going to communicate in HTML.

As the Internet became more popular, engineers found another problem. How could they tell the difference between the different organizations that were using the Internet?

Many schools today have 'computer rooms' where students can learn and practise their computer skills. A computer with Internet access can be a valuable research tool.

Internet addresses

Think for a moment about what is in a library. Fiction books are in one part of the library. Non-fiction books are in another part and other reference books, such as encyclopedias, have their spaces, too. All the books are library books, but they are all different. They are classified, or identified, by the type of book they are, as well as by their subject and author.

Saying that all organizations that use the Internet are the same is like saying all library books are the same. This is not the case. With so many different **networks** trying to talk with each other, engineers needed to identify, or classify, them. They needed a common filing system that

The Internet provides access to the resources found in hundreds of libraries like this one.

26

would help classify the different kinds of groups that were linked to the Internet. The classification system they created is called the domain naming system (DNS).

The domain name identifies the 'owner' of the website as well as the category it belongs to. Letters at the end of each Internet address indicate this category and are known as the TLD (top level domain). By looking at the TLD of an Internet address you can tell what type, or category, of website it will be.

The most common TLD is 'com,' which is short for commercial. This indicates that the domain name is registered to a business, or commercial organization (anywhere in the world) for the purpose of earning money. The TLD 'co.uk' indicates a commercial organization in the UK.

The domain naming system makes sure that each time you enter a URL (Internet address) you arrive at the right website.

The TLD 'org' is short for organization, or, more specifically, a non-profit organization. Organizations such as museums and charities use this TLD in their domain names, as they are not run just to make money or a profit.

Other TLDs include 'gov', which is used for government organizations. In Australia and the USA, the TLD 'edu' is used to indicate an educational institution. In the UK, schools use the TLD 'sch' and universities and colleges use 'ac' (for academic).

TLDs can also refer to the country in which the organization that created the website, is located. For example, 'au' refers to Australia, and 'uk' refers to the UK. So, if you see a website that ends with the TLD '.gov.uk', for example, you know that you are looking at a website belonging to a government organization in the UK.

Techno Tip

The Internet was originally designed in part to provide a communications network that would work even if some of the sites were destroyed by nuclear attack. If the most direct route was not available, devices called 'routers' would direct messages around the Internet using different routes.

The early Internet was used by computer experts, engineers, scientists and librarians. There were no home or office personal computers in those days, only mainframe computers. The Internet was not user-friendly and anyone who used it, had to learn a very complex system.

A website's entire address is called the uniform (or universal) resource locator, or URL. All URLs begin the same way – http://. This is followed by more letters and symbols. The diagram below shows you the different parts of a website address.

These letters tell your computer to go to a website. All URLs begin with the letters http followed by a colon and two forward slashes.

These letters represent part of the domain name. In this example, the letters nasa stand for National Aeronautics and Space Administration.

Many URLs include www.

These letters indicate the top level domain, or TLD. This describes the kind of site you are visiting. In this example, gov stands for government.

No two websites have exactly the same URL. Each URL is registered, or recorded, by an organization called the Internet **Network** Information Centre, or InterNIC.

Computers develop a face

In the 1980s, people began buying computers to use in their homes. However, these early personal computers, or PCs, were expensive and difficult to use.

Not many people used or understood the early PCs. One mistyped letter or symbol often made early computers crash, or stop running. Only people with lots of training used the first computers.

In the mid-1980s computers began to change. They began to have a new look. The dark screen was replaced with a friendly 'face.' This friendly face is called a GUI (gooey), or graphical user **interface**. The GUI is what you see on the monitor when you turn on your computer.

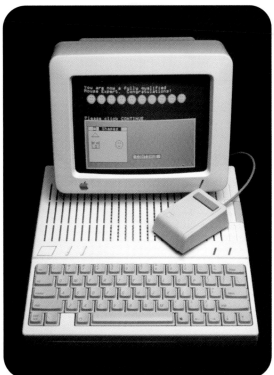

The first PCs were nowhere near as easy to use, or 'user-friendly', as today's modern PCs. They also had only a fraction of the computing power.

Today's GUI has a **desktop**, with **icons** (or buttons) or menus that allow you to choose and open different programs. These programs can be opened up on the screen in **windows**. The GUI was a leap forward for computer users and the Internet. It was easy to understand, even for people who were not engineers or scientists. More and more people began to use computers, especially to access the Internet, or go 'online.'

Among their many uses, for work and school, PCs today are also home entertainment centres on which you can play games, watch films and listen to music.

The world online

By 1987, there were 10,000 **networks** around the world. In 1989, there were 100,000 networks – the Internet grew ten times larger in just two years.

In 1991, the US government opened the Internet to everyone. People who had the right **hardware** and **software** joined. Small networks linked with large networks and soon, the Internet was growing at an amazing rate. Many businesses, organizations and individuals started using the Internet. All over the world people were getting online to exchange messages, news and information.

There are many online activities that a family can enjoy together.

The Internet becomes the Web

Most children today are growing up in a world where the Internet is part of everyday life. Perhaps that is why they seem to find it easier to use, than some of their parents or teachers do.

When most people think of the Internet, they think of the Web or World Wide Web – but the Web and the Internet are different. The Internet is a system of computers and programs that began in the early 1960s. The Web was created 30 years later. It is an information system that works on the Internet.

Until 1991, the Internet did not work in the same way it does today. Most people who used it were computer professionals and researchers. Although hypertext made it possible for computers to 'talk' to each other, some networks still could not talk to other networks. A British scientist named Tim Berners-Lee designed software that made it possible for more networks around

the world to link to the Internet. His **software** created the Internet addresses known as URLs. Those addresses became the foundation for the World Wide Web.

Another software, called Mosaic, took the Internet a step further. The Mosaic GUI was an **interface** for the Web. This interface allowed computer users to access documents or web pages by using a browser. A browser is a type of software that locates and displays web pages.

With access becoming easier, people started building websites on the Web. What are websites? A website is a collection of web pages. A web page is the pictures and text you see on a single page when you visit a website. Most websites have a home page that describes what you will find on the site. Sometimes websites offer a site map, which will show you how to move around the site and what to find there.

Although every home page looks different, they all usually welcome you to the site and give you an idea of what information it contains.

Web designers are people who make or build web pages. They may build one page, or many pages. When there is more than one page, designers link, or connect, the pages. Together, all the pages make a website. A designer can also create links from one website to another. These links are called 'hyperlinks'.

Web page designers use special computer languages based on hypertext to build web pages. These languages tell the computers how to show the words and pictures on a web page. It is also these languages that are used to create hyperlinks. The way a web page looks, and is used, will be the same – no matter where in the world it is being accessed from.

Techno Tip

A home page is usually the place to start when you are designing your own website. Type the following into a text document:

```
<html>
<title>This is the title of the page</title>
<body>
This is my home page!
</body>
</html>
```

Give your document a name, and save it with an .html extension. For example 'homepage.html'. Now open your Internet browser. When you open your document in the browser (go to 'file', 'open' and select your document) it should say 'This is my homepage!'.

As more and different people started building and designing websites, the Web became a much more interesting and exciting place. People could now easily share information and opinions on their hobbies, from sports to music. More and more people began to use the Web for research, not only for work or school, but also for things such as family history. People who love computer games discovered they could play together over the Web.

Researching family histories has become a popular use of the Web.

The Web did more than bring together people with similar interests. The Web was also growing into the world's largest community. It became a useful tool for learning about different cultures around the world and accessing information that was previously unavailable or difficult to get hold of. Some people think the Web has brought about an 'information revolution'.

The world's shopping centre

As access to the Web became easier during the 1990s, businesses began to look at the Web more closely. People began to imagine new ways to do business. All they needed was a place on the Web to call their own.

Soon businesses everywhere wanted their own websites. They used the Web to sell products and services. New businesses began, to take advantage of the new technology.

As the number of businesses and customers on the Web grew, the Internet developed. As well as being a global communication tool it was now the world's shopping centre. Businesses used the Web to advertise. Customers could shop 24 hours a day, 7 days a week. This new way of buying and selling goods is called e-commerce, or electronic business.

People no longer have to leave home to do their shopping. With most big supermarkets providing online shopping, you can now choose your food on the Web and have it delivered to your door.

The Internet and the Web today

How big is the Internet today? In 2002 there were over 500 million Internet users around the world. Of those 500 million users, over 30 million were in the UK, and over 5 million in Australia. The USA has the most Internet users of any country in the world.

The online world is filled with information, communities and businesses. The Web grows and changes every day. New people connect to it and new websites are being created and updated all the time.

Internet cafes are becoming more and more popular around the world as places where people can use a computer and access the Internet for a small fee.

As more people around the world have access to the Internet, the global market gets bigger. Thousands of new users go online every day. If they don't own computers, people find other ways to get online. In many countries, for example, people visit Internet cafes. These cafes sell more than drinks and snacks. They sell computer-time. People can use the Internet there to surf the Web or send and receive emails.

Using computers and the Internet as a way of exchanging and listening to music is becoming more popular as the technology for doing so becomes cheaper and easier to use.

What's happening online?

Large numbers of people around the world visit the Web each year. What do they do there? They learn and have fun. They shop and listen to music. They watch films and read books.

The Web today is also a valuable tool in classrooms around the world. Students everywhere can connect to the Web and find information to help them with their studies. Real-time video with music and sound effects are found on different entertainment and educational websites.

Searching the Web

So, once you're on the Web, how do you find what you're looking for? You can use a search engine. A search engine is an online tool that helps you move around the Web. Tell the search engine what you are looking for, and it will take you there.

How? You type in words called keywords. Keywords are words that describe briefly what you are looking for. For example, if you are looking for information about whales, you would type the keyword 'whales' into the search engine. Then, the engine looks through pages of the Web to find what you want. If it can't find what you want, it tells you. If it does find what you want, a list of links to websites that give information about whales will appear on your computer screen. When you click from link to link, you are surfing the net.

There are sites on the Internet that allow you to track the progress of animal and nature conservation projects and even to view endangered species, such as the humpback whale, in their natural habitat.

You might start by visiting the National Trust online and planning a trip. Or you might take a tour of The Virtual Gallery at the Natural History Museum or take a closer look inside the Sydney Opera House. You might try exploring space via NASA's website. There, you can actually take a tour of the inside of the International Space Station as well as looking at the most up-to-date images of the planets and stars.

Some sites combine education and entertainment. Such sites link you with games to play and lots of other learning activities. For example, why not play one of the games at www.creative-chemistry.org.uk and combine science with fun?

It does take some time and practice to search the Web effectively. Once you have learned the basics, you'll be able to find out about almost anything you can think of! No matter what you want to know, the Web can probably give you the answers. If you don't have a computer at home or an Internet connection, you can probably get online at school or a local library.

Techno Tip

Scientists are exploring the possibility of expanding the internet into space – linking the Web with spacecraft, sattelites and robotic probes. Sending email between planets would have its own set of challenges. Sometimes another planet would be blocking the signal.

Who's in charge of the Internet?

Because the Internet is electronic, it crosses many boundaries. This means that no country or group has power over it. Each computer **network** within the Internet has its own managers and owners. Each owner or manager sets rules and guidelines for users within its network. The US government used to control the development of the Internet – but today it controls only its own networks and websites.

The Web runs on the 'honour system'. This means that individuals and companies must be responsible for the information they are providing on their websites. If something is thought to be wrong in the real world – it is wrong on the Web.

People on the Web try and encourage 'netiquette'. This means being polite on the Internet. Sometimes people write things in email that they wouldn't say in person.

The use of passwords (or password protection) is one way of trying to stop 'cybercrime' (crimes committed using computers).

When you email, keep in mind that there is a person with feelings at the other end. Some network managers can throw a misbehaving emailer off the Web if they are not following the rules of good behaviour!

As with most things you do, a parent, a teacher, or a responsible adult should always be aware of what you are doing when you are online.

Techno Tip

Here are some guidelines to help you surf safely.

DO NOT give out:

✗ *pictures of you or your family*

✗ *your address*

✗ *your phone number*

✗ *personal information such as what you look like, or where you go to school.*

DO NOT share your passwords with anybody.

NEVER click on an email attachment or web link unless you know the sender.

DO NOT join a chat room without talking it over with your parents or a guardian.

NEVER agree to meet someone you have met on the web. That can be very dangerous.

Some people can now access the Internet through their television.

The Internet and the future

Television, video, film, computers and the Internet seem to be coming together. Instead of using separate machines for TV, telephone, Internet, fax, music and films, the future may bring one machine that meets all these needs. What do you think this computer of the future would look like?

The Internet of the future will bring more opportunities for distance learning, or learning over the Internet. Many more schools and colleges could offer online classes. Think of what it would be like to connect with your class and teacher over the Internet. You could talk with your teacher through a video screen on your computer and never even leave home!

The Internet is changing how we work and live. Thanks to the Internet, people all over the world can share ideas, discoveries and information. The Internet allows us to learn more about each other. Websites on the Internet come

from many places around the world. They are written in different languages and can show us different ways of life.

The dreams of early Internet pioneers like Bob Taylor are becoming real. People start to feel like global citizens when they travel online. The Internet can make the people of the world seem like next-door neighbours.

The Internet can be a gateway to a richer life if you use it as a positive tool. You can think of the Internet as a huge classroom that holds all the world's information. A computer, a phone line and the click of a mouse lets you in!

Wherever you live in the world – as long as you have the right equipment – the Internet can connect you to people, places and information.

Resources

Further reading

Building a school website: a hands on project for teachers and kids, Wanda Wigglebits (Duomo Press, 2000)

Communicating Today: Internet and email, Chris Oxlade (Heinemann Library, 2001)

The best Internet sites for kids, (Hodder & Stoughton Educational, 2002)

The Virgin Internet guide for kids, Davey Winder (Virgin Books, 2000)

Interesting and useful websites

NASA: *http://www.nasa.gov*

The National Trust: *http://www.nationaltrust.org.uk*

Creative Chemistry: *http://www.creative-chemistry.org.uk*

Internet for Kids: *http://www.internet4kids.com*

Childrens BBC: *http://www.bbc.co.uk/cbbc* and **BBC Schools**: *http://www.bbc.co.uk/schools*

Some search engines:

www.google.co.uk

www.yahoo.com or *www.yahooligans.com*

www.webwombat.com.au

Disclaimer
All the Internet addresses (URLs) given in this book were valid at the time of going to press. However, due to the dynamic nature of the Internet, some addresses may have changed, or sites may have ceased to exist since publication. While the author and publishers regret any inconvenience this may cause readers, no responsibility for any such changes can be accepted by either the author or the publishers.

Glossary

desktop area of the display screen where icons are grouped (see icons)

eccentric different, slightly strange behaviour. A person is called eccentric if they behave in this way.

hardware machines, wiring and other physical parts of a computer (for example, display screen (monitor), keyboard, printer etc.)

hub device that directs messages between the server and computers attached to a network

icon small pictures that stand for commands, files or programs. By moving the cursor to the icon and double-clicking your mouse, you can carry out commands, open files and run programs.

Interface device or program that lets a user communicate with a computer, or connects two pieces of hardware or software

Intranet network based on the same technology as the Internet, belonging to an organization and available only to its members. An Intranet's web pages look and act in the same way as those on the Internet and are a way of sharing information within an organization.

mainframe very large, expensive computer that can support hundreds or thousands of users at a time

network group of two or more computers (hardware and software) linked together

server computer or computer program that manages access to a network's resources (information, files and programs)

software computer instructions or information. Software is stored and displayed using hardware.

telecommunication communication of sounds, signals or pictures over a distance. Telephones, radio and television are examples of telecommunication.

transmit pass on or send out (for example, an electrical signal or TV or radio programme)

window area of the display screen in which you can run programs or display files and documents. More than one window can be open at a time and you can move, enlarge and reduce them using your mouse.

Index